BIBLICAL CHRISTIANITY IN AFRICA

Theological Perspectives in Africa: No. 2

BIBLICAL CHRISTIANITY
IN AFRICA
a collection of
papers and addresses

Byang H. Kato, B.D., S.T.M., Th.D.

AFRICA CHRISTIAN PRESS

© AFRICA CHRISTIAN PRESS

First edition 1985

ISBN 9964 87 793 5

Theological Perspectives in Africa

A series of monographs designed to provide, in handy format,
theological perspectives on vital issues facing Christianity
in Africa today.

General Editor
Tite Tiénou
(Bobo Dioulasso, Upper Volta)

Consulting Editors
David Gitari (Embu, Kenya)
Cornelius Olowola (Igbaja, Nigeria)

Titles issued to date:
1 Tite Tiénou, The Theological Task of the Church in Africa
2 Byang Kato, Biblical Christianity in Africa

Trade orders to:
Nigeria: Challenge Bookshops, PMB 12256, Lagos, and Fellent
Ltd, PO Box 5923, Lagos
Kenya: Keswick Bookshop, PO Box 10242, Nairobi, and Kesho
Publications, PO Box 30351, Nairobi
S. Africa: ACLA, PO Box 332, Roodepoort 1725, Transvaal
Australia: Bookhouse, PO Box 115, Flemington Markets,
NSW 2129
UK: ACP, 49 Thornbury Road, Isleworth, Middlesex TW7 4LE

All other countries:
Africa Christian Press, PO Box 30, Achimota, Ghana, W. Africa

Phototypeset by Nuprint Services Ltd, Harpenden, Herts and printed
in England by Arrowsmith, Bristol

CONTENTS

Preface   vii

Sources   ix

1 Theological anemia in Africa (February 1973)   11

2 The theology of eternal salvation (January 1974)   15

3 Contextualization and religious syncretism in Africa (July 1974) 23

4 Christianity as an African religion (April 1975)   32

5 Theological issues in Africa (September 1975)   40

Suggestions for further reading   54

The views expressed in these monographs are those of each author and do not necessarily represent those of the editors of the series or of the publisher.

PREFACE

Byang Kato was a man of experience and ability. Born in Nigeria in 1936, he was raised in tribal religion by his parents. Under the ministry of a local African teacher he became a Christian and later entered Igbaja Bible College to train for Christian work. After graduation, Kato served as a youth leader, as a counsellor with *African Challenge* magazine, and as a Bible school teacher. He attended London Bible College, and in 1966 obtained the University of London B.D. degree. On his return to Nigeria, he was elected general secretary of the Evangelical Churches of West Africa (ECWA). In 1971 Kato completed his S.T.M. degree, and in 1974 his Th.D. degree, both from Dallas Theological Seminary. In 1973 he was elected general secretary of the Association of Evangelicals of Africa and Madagascar (AEAM). In 1974 he was chosen as vice-president of the World Evangelical Fellowship (WEF), and in 1975 appointed chairman of its theological commission. In December 1975 the Christian world was shocked to learn of his accidental death by drowning while on holiday.

Byang Kato was a man of commitment and vision. His life was dominated by his devotion to Jesus Christ, and by his love for Africa. His whole ministry was directed toward the rootage and growth of biblical Christianity on the continent. He was especially troubled by evidence of theological indifference and deviation within the church, and sought by every means to strengthen theological life within Africa. In his continental and his international leadership roles, Kato endeavoured to rally Christians to the theological tasks confronting the cause of Christ today. He wrote and spoke, he encouraged and challenged, and he dreamed dreams. From his vision arose an AEAM commission to give theological direction among Christians in Africa, an accrediting service for African theological colleges, and two post-graduate schools of theology, one for francophone Africa and the other for anglophone Africa. His vision continues to influence those who give leadership today in theological life in Africa.

At the time of his death in 1975, Kato had published one book and completed two smaller pamphlets. But much of Kato's material was left in generally unorganized and unedited form. Several of his papers were published as articles during his lifetime, and others appeared afterward. These often exist in several different published and unpublished versions. In order to meet the continuing interest in Byang Kato, and in what he wrote and said, we have here gathered together in handy and easily accessible form five major papers and addresses that Byang Kato gave between 1973 and 1975. These have been edited, sometimes abbreviated, and – where different versions exist – also collated. Footnotes have been left as they appear in Kato's original text. Full reference for the sources of these materials is given on pages ix, x.

While these materials are of historical interest, in charting an important aspect of recent Christian theological life in Africa, they are also of abiding relevance for all those who today share Kato's vision for a Christianity on the continent that will be, in Kato's phrase, 'truly biblical and truly African'.

Tite Tiénou
Upper Volta

SOURCES

THEOLOGICAL ANEMIA IN AFRICA

Part of this material formed the paper 'Theological Trends in Africa Today' presented 4 February 1973 to the Third General Assembly of the Association of Evangelicals of Africa and Madagascar, at Limuru, Kenya, and published in *Perception* No. 1 (March 1974). The revised and expanded version here presented first appeared in *Africa Now* No. 76 (September–October 1974) under the title 'We are at a Turning Point in Africa's Church History'.

THE THEOLOGY OF ETERNAL SALVATION

A paper first read at a theological consultation at Limuru, Kenya, sponsored by the Theological Commission of the Association of Evangelicals of Africa and Madagascar, 8–10 January 1974, and later published in *Perception* No. 14 (October 1978).

CONTEXTUALIZATION AND RELIGIOUS SYNCRETISM IN AFRICA

An address given at the International Congress on World Evangelization, Lausanne, Switzerland, 16–25 July 1974, and subsequently published in *Let the Earth Hear His Voice*, ed. J. D. Douglas (Minneapolis, 1975) 1216–1223, under the title 'The Gospel, Cultural Context and Religious Syncretism'.

CHRISTIANITY AS AN AFRICA RELIGION

First given as an address at the Nigerian 'National Congress on Evangelization', University of Ife, Ile-Ife, Nigeria, 21 April 1975. First published in *Perception* No. 16 (May 1979).

THEOLOGICAL ISSUES IN AFRICA

Part of this material was first given as a public lecture at the University of Nairobi in Kenya, 27 September 1975, under the title 'Black Theology and African Theology'. In that form it appeared in *Theological News* viii.1 (January 1976), and later in *Perception* No. 6 (October 1976) and the *Evangelical Review of Theology* i.1 (October 1977). The expanded version here presented appeared first as two connected articles in *Bibliotheca Sacra* cxxxiii.530 (April–June 1976) and cxxxiii.531 (July–September 1976), under the titles 'Theological Issues in Africa' and 'An Evaluation of Black Theology'.

1

THEOLOGICAL ANEMIA
IN AFRICA

(February 1973)

Biblical Christianity in Africa is being threatened by syncretism, universalism, and Christo-paganism. The spiritual battle for Africa during this decade will be fought, therefore, largely on theological grounds. But the church is generally unprepared for the challenge because of its theological and biblical ignorance. There are at least two major reasons for this.

First, the church was not prepared for the unexpected phenomenal growth evident today. Dr. Raymond Davis of the Sudan Interior Mission bears this out in his statement: 'Neither missions nor the church in Africa accurately anticipated and consequently planned for the magnitude of today's demands. We face an unexpected crisis in many areas of Africa today as the result of great and unprecedented church expansion.'

Secondly, theological ignorance or neglect by our forebearers. Thank God the picture is changing, but the fact remains that the church in Africa is suffering from theological anemia due to the failures of the past. Professor John Mbiti of Kenya has rightly observed: 'Mission Christianity was not from the start prepared to face a serious encounter with either traditional religions and philosophy or the modern changes taking place in Africa. The church here now finds itself in the situation of trying to exist without a theology.'

In a frantic mood, African theologians have embarked upon the task of formulating a theology for Africa. That Africans have a unique contribution to make to theological debates is undeniable. But the brand of theology being proposed includes features such as: the use of sources other than the Scriptures as in equal standing with the revealed Word of God, the possibility of salvation in African traditional religions, and a strong emphasis on things African for their own sake. Dr. J. K. Agbeti of Ghana states: 'Materials about African religion are being collected and collated regionally. From these regional sources could grow later a religion which could be truly called African Religion. It will be from this source that an African theology may be developed.'

This great enthusiasm about African religions is one sad danger evident in some of the formulations by these theologians. Many of them fail to see the unique nature of Biblical revelation. They may hold the view of a unique Christ, but at the same time assume an errant Bible. But how can I know for sure about Jesus Christ in an errant Bible? Inerrant authoritative Scriptures can alone give us reliable facts about Jesus Christ and man's relationship to Him.

Africans need to formulate theological concepts in the language of Africa. But theology itself in its essence must be left alone. The Bible must remain the basic source of Christian theology. Evangelical Christians know of only one theology–Biblical theology–though it may be expressed in the context of each cultural milieu.

Most African universities have a department of religions. The basic philosophy of many of these departments appears to be a search for peaceful coexistence between religions in Africa. The prevailing attitude is that Christianity is only one of the many ways of salvation, though it may be understood as a fulfilment of all other religions. The influence of these university departments is going to grow.

The ecumenical movement is exerting enormous pressures within Africa. Dr. George Peters says: 'It is evident that evangelical missions have not taken the ecumenical movement seriously enough. The evangelical younger churches as a whole are not able to withstand the pressure and the play on nationalism on the one hand, and the promises and enticements on the other. Bold and tactful indoctrination, rather than cold denunciation, is urgently needed.' The primary goal of ecumenism, according to R. B. Lightner, is 'world-wide cooperation and fellowship among all religious bodies regardless of doctrinal agreement.' Since the goal is union, doctrine is played down. The constant cry is, 'Doctrine divides, service unites.' 'The real danger to the ecumenical movement in Africa', Professor John Mbiti warns, 'lies in attaining a church unity which then becomes a theological stagnation for those who subscribe or belong to it.'

Ecumenism offers many attractions. There is an emphasis on nationalism, and the claim of being the champion of unity–attractive factors to the governments of Africa. There is also the emphasis on leadership training. Nearly a hundred Asian and African students are enrolled in liberal seminaries in the USA through ecumenical scholarship programmes. The World Council of Churches spends $3 million every five years on students from the Third World. Ecumenism has already asserted great influence in Africa.

The evangelical church in Africa, as a whole, is at a historic turning point. Her future will be decided by what happens in the next few years. If she is to meet the challenge, theological training must be strengthened. Every possible means of teaching the church must be expanded and deepened and strengthened. This must be done at every level, but particularly at the highest leadership levels. While it is true that Africa needs help of many kinds, it is in the area of church leadership that evangelicals are most lacking. This is an expensive proposition, but it must be done. Top priorities include the following:

Seminary training. It is true that Jesus Christ used humble, unlearned Galilean fishermen, but it is also true that He commissioned well-educated men such as Paul and Luke, and gave them vital roles in defining and defending the church's doctrinal position. More seminary-level theological schools need to be established in Africa. The present ones need to be strengthened, and their teaching made accessible to many more church leaders.

Graduate training. There is not a single evangelical theological school in Africa that offers a post-graduate degree, in a continent whose 'Christian' population now exceeds 100 million. Qualified Christian men and women looking for advanced training have nowhere to turn within Africa. The recently-formed Theological Commission, of the Association of Evangelicals of Africa and Madagascar, is actively seeking to establish two such schools, one in English and one in French. They will cost money that Africa's evangelicals do not have.

Scholarship programmes. At this stage, when churches are just emerging in many ways, many Africans must be sent abroad for theological studies. With few exceptions the policy has been to send men overseas only for training they cannot get within their own country. But there are many qualified students who cannot be sent overseas because there is not the money to send them. Funds for scholarships within Africa are sorely needed.

Publications. Most theological writing by African authors, at an academic level, is by liberals or those sympathetic to liberal theology.

Africa needs an indigenous evangelical theological journal, along the lines of *Christianity Today*.

Theological society. A theological society should be formed, to provide evangelical African theologians with a platform for propagating sound theology and gaining a hearing in educated circles.

There is no way that Africa can adequately finance these needs. At this point in our history, the church of Jesus Christ worldwide must share its bounty with those members of the body that are in special need. It is very important that missionary-minded Christians be alerted to the danger facing the tremendous work they have built in Africa over the years. As they have given to build in the past, it is needful that they give now to protect the future. The emphasis must be upon seeing that the Lord's work moves ahead, regardless of who is doing it, missionary or African. I put forward the suggestion that for every missionary sent to Africa by churches in the West, those churches undertake the training of at least one African for the church in Africa.

2

THE THEOLOGY OF ETERNAL SALVATION

(January 1974)

We are engaged in a battle for the survival of sound biblical Christianity in the African continent. Should the revealed Christian faith be sacrificed at the altar of syncretistic universalism, in the guise of contextualization? Should the church in Africa exchange eternal values of the *Kerygma* for 'one morsel'? Or is the evangelical concern for eternal values nothing more than a 'pie-in-the-sky by-and-by' theology? These are issues that require attention in Africa today.

1. The Human Crisis

Some months ago I fell sick while speaking at a church meeting. It was a sudden stomach seizure. I was rushed to the hospital. At the emergency room they took a series of tests to determine the root cause of my illness. I was anxious to get some medicine. But after several tests the doctor sent me home — without a single pill. He could not find the cause, and so he would not give a treatment. Indeed no doctor worthy of the name would give a prescription without a proper diagnosis. We can learn something from this, as we face the far weightier questions of the human crisis. Correct diagnosis is necessary before treatment. A wrong theology of sin necessarily ends up with a wrong concept of salvation.

Exploitation, disease, abject poverty, and deprivation of the basic necessities of life have been the lot of the majority of African people. But what is the root cause of these human tragedies? Would man's problems be solved after alleviation of physical suffering and material deprivation? Is putting clothes on a man's back and food in his stomach the way to solve man's basic need? Is political liberation the

15

final answer? History counters any positive answers to these questions. Man's root problem is beyond these issues.

The high rate of crime, the utter discontentment, and the emptiness prevalent in the industrialized nations of the world is a sad commentary on our Lord's words that 'man's life does not consist in what he has'. Every inch of the African continent may be liberated from foreign domination, every family may have two cars in the garage, and every African may be a college graduate, but that still will not save the African from his fundamental dilemma. These current ills will only be replaced with new and probably worse tragedies.

Francis Schaeffer is stating universal truth when he says: 'Since there are aspirations which separate man from his impersonal universe, man then faces at the heart of his being a terrible, cosmic, final alienation. He drowns in cosmic alienation, for there is nothing in the universe to fulfil him in all that there is.'[1] The nature of man's fundamental dilemma does not lie in mere physical suffering. It does not lie primarily in horizontal relationships with his fellow man. All human tragedies, be they sickness, poverty, or exploitation, are mere symptoms of the root cause, which the Bible calls sin.

It is very sad to note that some key church leaders in Africa take these symtoms for the root causes. Rev. Canon Burgess Carr, general secretary of the All Africa Conference of Churches, tells the overseas press:

> The most urgent task of the churches in Africa is to ensure that we keep the initiative at this critical moment in the development of our peoples as they struggle for complete liberation. And I say complete liberation because I'm thinking of liberation in the broadest sense, which is not only the liberation from political, colonial domination but the liberation from economic slavery, the liberation from all the human indignities that we suffer across that continent of black Africa.[2]

Not once in his interview did I notice Canon Carr mention sin or its synonym.

After an exhaustive ministry to the sick, teaching and preaching to a less responsive audience, Jesus Christ did not cry for more health officers and social workers. Rather, 'He felt compassion for them, because they were distressed and downcast like sheep without a shepherd. Then he said to his disciples, "The harvest is plentiful but the workers are few. Therefore beseech the Lord of the harvest to send out workers into his harvest"' (Matthew 9:36–38). In a similar vein the Lord wept for the cities socially and economically well cared for, but still spiritually depraved. 'Then he began to reproach the cities in which most of his miracles were done, because they did not repent... Woe to you, Chorazin!' (Matthew 11:20–21). He then offered a warm invitation for true liberation: 'Come to me, all who are weary and heavy laden, and I will give you rest' (Matthew 11:28). The affluent city of Jerusalem broke the heart of the Saviour because of spiritual degradation (Luke 19:41). The sons of Abraham were not aware that they were under eternal bondage and had need of him who said, 'If therefore the Son shall make you free, you shall be free indeed' (John 8:36).

Man's fundamental dilemma is alienation from God. The historical account of Genesis 3 gives the root cause of all sufferings here and in the life to come. As man has armed himself in rebellion against his Creator, self-assertion or autonomy has become the dominant factor of his being. James says, 'What is the source of quarrels and conflicts among you? Is not the source your pleasures that wage war in your members?' (James 4:1). After giving a long catalogue of wicked human deeds, Paul sums up: 'For all have sinned and fall short of the glory of God' (Romans 3:23). All human tragedies come as a result of sin.

2. Redemptive Revelation

If man's fundamental dilemma is sin which is the root cause of suffering, to deal with sin will be the logical way to deal with the dilemma. The basic presupposition is that man has sinned against God. But how does man know about God unless God has given Himself to be known? That God has indeed revealed Himself to all mankind is evident in miracles, which postulate other-worldness; nature and history, which indicate a great Master Designer and Operator; and world religions, which show man's craving for something beyond himself. The traditional arguments for the existence of God – cosmological, teleological, ontological, and anthropological – point not only to the possibility but to the strong probability of 'the God who is there and is not silent'.

It is rather naive on the part of some scholars of the past to have denied the possibility of the knowledge of God among Africans. That the 'heathen' adherent has some awareness of his Creator is an axiom, since every human being has been made in the image of God (Genesis 1:27). The original fall, admittedly, has distorted that image of God; therefore the unregenerate man may be said to be 'dead in sins and trespasses' (Ephesians 2:1). But the image of God in man is not destroyed in the sense of being eradicated; if it were, man would be deprived of a sense of morality, a will to decide, and an ability to make rational choices. He would be guided by instinct rather than by reason. Man everywhere and in any age is able to have awareness of God.

Another source for God's revelation is nature. When the Apostle Paul declared that God 'did not leave Himself without a witness' (Acts 14:17), he was referring to the wonderful works of God in nature, and His provision for the righteous and the wicked. That God has revealed Himself to men everywhere is conclusive from the human point of view and from what is given in the Scriptures. Although Professor John Mbiti took too much liberty to systematize the thinking of the worshippers in African traditional religions, nevertheless his book *Concepts of God in Africa* indicates the fact of some knowledge of God in traditional Africa.

The crucial question which confronts us is whether there can be salvation in such general revelation. Going back farther, how clear are the 'heathen' in their interpretation of God's general revelation? Although every effort has been put into bringing African traditional religions in line with Christian revelation, it is evident that contradictions and fears are basic factors in worship. Bishop Stephen Neill has rightly observed: 'No one can understand the real situation of primitive man without taking serious account of the three motive powers of shame, guilt and fear.'[3] The many myths that take God away from human affairs and enthrone man to be served by women and children, are indicative of the distortion of man's knowledge of God. The Apostle Paul does admit the possibility of the knowledge of God among the 'heathen'. But he also affirms that man's total depravity has led him down the path of idolatry (Romans 1:20–32).

The most we can say of the African traditional worshipper is that there is a craving for a spiritual reality. This craving is turned into idolatry as man turns to worship creation rather than the Creator. Unfortunately some African theologians seek to justify this idolatry by associating the idols with God Himself. Professor Bolaji Idowu writes: 'From the point of view of the theology of African traditional religion, it will not be correct to say that the divinities were created. It will be correct to say that they were brought into being, or that they came into being in the nature of things with regard to divine ordering of the universe.... The Divinities are derivatives from Deity.'[4] In biblical perspective, while this craving for some spiritual reality may be considered an evidence of general revelation, the worship itself must be seen as an abuse of that revelation.

General revelation does not, and cannot, bring salvation. This is not due to any limitation on the part of God, but rather to the historical fall of man. G. C. Berkouwer writes: 'When we speak of insufficiency, we certainly do not intend to cast any reflection on the divine act of revelation in this general revelation. On the contrary, it only points to human guilt and blindness. This insufficiency is not a deficiency of revelation, but it is a deficiency which is historically determined, i.e. in connection with the fall of man.'[5]

If the best that religious pluralism can do is demonstrate the thirst in the human soul, it stands to reason that God's special revelation in Jesus Christ alone can save. Besides making ultimate claims about Himself – the Way, the Truth, the Life, the Door, the Good Shepherd, One with the Father – and justifying all of them, the Son of God also invites all men to come to Him for salvation (Matthew 11:28–29). Peter, through the Holy Spirit, declared, 'And there is salvation in no one else; for there is no other name under heaven that has been given among men, by which we must be saved' (Acts 4:12). The Apostle Paul affirms, 'Therefore also God highly exalted him, and bestowed on him the name which is above every name, that at the name of Jesus every knee should bow, of those who are in heaven, and on earth and under the earth' (Philippians 2:9–10).

The unique revelation of God in Christ is clear – only One Way of salvation for all men, and that is through Jesus Christ. Stephen Neill emphasizes: 'For the human sickness there is one specific remedy, and this is it. There is no other.'[6] Some people consider this claim a type of cultural pride and neocolonialism. Neill further observes, 'Naturally to the non-Christian hearer this must sound like crazy megalomania and religious imperialism of the very worst kind.'[7] But it must be recalled that Christ and His followers suffered worse accusations before the sinful world. Can Christ's servant expect anything better?

We may sum up in this manner. God has revealed Himself in two ways – *general* non-redemptive revelation on the one hand, and *special* redemptive revelation on the other. In the context of African traditional religions, the worship is merely an indication of an honest craving for God, which can be fulfilled only in biblical revelation through the incarnate Christ who died and rose again. This should be the preoccupation of the church in Africa.

3. The Person of Christ

Professor John Mbiti has rightly affirmed, 'The uniqueness of Christianity is in Jesus Christ. He is the stumbling block of all ideologies and religious systems; and even if some of His teaching may overlap with what they teach and proclaim, His Person is greater than can be contained in a religion or ideology. He is "the Man for others" and yet beyond them.'[8] At the same time in other writings he says, 'Jesus may have accepted current notions about Gehenna without necessarily endorsing them all.'[9] He further states, 'The New Testament is explicit that Jesus never promised us a heavenly utopia, but only His own self and His own companionship both in time and beyond, both in space and beyond.'[10] While Jesus Christ affirms eternal suffering in hell (Matthew 10:28; 18:9; 23:15,33; Luke 12:5), Mbiti spiritualizes it into symbolism by saying, 'If people are threatened with being cast into a lake of fire in the next life, the effectiveness of the symbol is largely lost and the Christian Gospel is reduced to negative threats which have no lasting impact upon those who receive or reject Christ.'[11] Thus, Mbiti fails to treat the teaching of Christ with the same seriousness he devotes to the unique role of Christ.

This is one example of how the Person of Christ and His work have been a stumbling block throughout the ages. Christological controversies date back to the time Christ was on earth. Religious leaders and government authorities were puzzled about this Son of God and Son of Man. It was only through the Holy Spirit that men like Peter could declare, 'Thou art the Christ, the Son of the living God' (Matthew 16:16). Even after the Father had authenticated the ultimate claims of the Incarnate Christ by raising Him from the dead and exalting Him at His right hand, the Person of Christ was still a real problem to His followers and to pagans of the early centuries of Christianity. The early apologists – Justin, Tatian, Athenagoras, Theophilus of Antioch – bravely wielded the sword against false teaching about Christ. But even some of them became victims of the heresies they sought to repudiate. As Berkhof explains: 'The Apologists did not have the biblical conception of the Logos, but one somewhat resembling that of Philo. To them the Logos, as He existed eternally in God, was simply the divine reason, without personal existence.'[12] Justin succumbed to the spirit of the age in declaring, 'We are taught that Christ is the first born of God, and we have shown above that He is the reason (Word) of whom the whole human race partake, and those who live according to reason are Christians, even though they are accounted atheists. Such were Socrates and Heraclitus among the Greeks, and those like them....'[13]

I once had a brief discussion with an African theologian who firmly stated that the Logos spirit was operative in African traditional religions. Therefore to deny salvation to these worshippers is to deny the working of God in their midst. Second century gnosticism has come back to life. As Christ has been depersonalized in liberal theology (e.g. Schleiermacher, Ritschl), the same tendency is rising in Africa today as some African theologians seek to glorify African traditional religions. But it must be maintained that Jesus Christ became incarnate as a particular person in time and history. John's use of Logos (John 1:1–7) was in that particular sense. The Word became flesh by assuming not only the form of man in general (Philippians 2:5–8), but by being born as a particular person in Bethlehem. This was necessary in view of the work He was going to do. He could be crucified in time and history only as a particular man. He died and rose as an individual to save each individual sinner.

Christological controversies did not end with His person. It may be agreed that the Incarnate Christ is God-Man eternally since He came to earth. But the question of His work could still remain an enigma. The historical debate on the atonement need not detain us. Suffice it to indicate that the substitutionary death of Christ for men everywhere at any time is the position held by most evangelical Christians. What poses a threat to Christian witness in Africa today is the meaning attached to the contemporary so-called 'Salvation Today' debate. The exponents of that view find salvation in people's experiences rather than in the objective revelation of God's written and Living Word.

Thomas Wieser has written, 'Unless we can understand and express the Gospel in connection with the contemporary social, political and cultural changes, individual salvation is meaningless.'[14] Writing of the various means that provide or express salvation, Wieser states, 'It will, therefore, be necessary to clarify which are important expressions and this may well be the crucial task for an international-ecumenical gathering on this theme. In preparation for this task the staff of the Commission are presently engaged in making a collection of texts taken from religious and secular literature. These represent different aspects of the contemporary experience of salvation which raise the same issues as we have recognized in the traditions incorporated in the scriptural writings.'[15] Perhaps it was in this spirit of searching for other possible ways of salvation that theologians and church leaders gathered together last year in Ibadan, Nigeria, to dialogue with worshippers of traditional religions. Since salvation is possible elsewhere than in Christ, the dialogue was hardly to promote evangelism.

But if biblical Christianity is to survive and flourish in Africa, we must hold fast the truth that man's fundamental problem is sin against God, and that salvation is only through Jesus Christ. We must hold to the uniqueness of Christian revelation through the written Word and through the Living Word. To seek salvation elsewhere than through the shed blood of Christ is heretical. It is the preaching of another gospel, which really is no gospel. As Donald Jacobs has put it, 'There is *no salvation outside of Christ*. If there would be, Christianity would be a lie.'[16] The work of Christ is alone fully sufficient for our redemption.

NOTES

1 Francis Schaeffer, *The Church at the End of the 20th Century,* 16.
2 *AACC Bulletin,* 26 June 1973.
3 Stephen Neill, *Christian Faith and Other Faiths,* 137.
4 E. Bolaji Idowu, *African Traditional Religion: A Definition,* 169.
5 G. C. Berkouwer, *General Revelation,* 132.
6 Stephen Neill, 17.
7 Ibid.
8 John S. Mbiti, *African Religions and Philosophy,* 363.
9 John S. Mbiti, *New Testament Eschatology in an African Background,* 66.
10 Ibid, 89.
11 Ibid, 70.
12 Louis Berkhof, *The History of Christian Doctrine,* 58.
13 Justin, *Apology* I. xlvi. 2–4.
14 *International Review of Mission* (July, 1971) 383.
15 Ibid, 388.
16 Donald Jacobs, *Christian Theology in Africa,* 6.

3

CONTEXTUALIZATION AND RELIGIOUS SYNCRETISM IN AFRICA

(July 1974)

'If I had a thousand lives I would give them to the service of Christ in Africa.' Robert Moffat uttered this passionate cry because he had a clear cut Gospel to proclaim, and Africa (as other parts of the world) was groping in complete darkness without Christ. This is not to deny God's general revelation through nature, conscience, history, and miracles. But it is to affirm that 'he who has the Son has life' (1 John 5:12). If there was a time in Africa when there was a need for a clear-cut Gospel, it is today. If there was a time when Christ's sons and daughters in Africa must be prepared to lay down their lives for the undiluted Gospel, it is today. It is, therefore, a great privilege for me to share with God's servants my understanding of the challenge which the Gospel faces in Africa in the areas of contextualization and syncretism.

1 Contextualization

'Contextualization' is a new term imported into theology to express a deeper concept than 'indigenization' ever does. I understand the term to mean making concepts or ideas relevant in a given situation. In reference to Christian practices, it is an effort to express the never changing Word of God in ever changing modes for relevance. Since the Gospel message is inspired but the mode of its expression is not, contextualization of the modes of expression is not only right but necessary. William Barclay has rightly stated:

> It is not Jesus' purpose that we should turn all men into one nation, but that there should be Christian Indians and Christian

23

Africans, whose unity lies in their Christianity. The oneness in
Christ is in Christ, and not in any external change. The unity in
Christ produces Christians whose Christianity transcends all
their local and racial differences; it produces men who are
friends with each other because they are friends with God; it
produces men who are one, because they meet in the presence
of God to whom they have access.

The New Testament has given us the pattern for cultural
adaptations. The incarnation itself is a form of contextualization. The
Son of God condescended to pitch His tent among us to make it
possible for us to be redeemed (John 1:14). The unapproachable
Yahweh, whom no man has seen and lived, has become the Object of
sight and touch through the incarnation (John 14:9; 1 John 1:1). The
moving hymn on the humiliation and exaltation of Jesus Christ the
Lord (Philippians 2:5–8) was evidently an incentive to the Apostle
Paul in his understanding of the ministry, to become 'all things to all
men'. This in turn should motivate us to make the Gospel relevant in
every situation everywhere, without compromising it.

Contextualization can take place in liturgy, dress, language, church
service, and any other form of expression of the Gospel truth. Musical
instruments such as organ and piano can be replaced or supplemented
with such indigenous and easily acquired instruments as drums,
cymbals, and cornstalk instruments. It must be borne in mind, of
course, that the sound of music must not drown the message. Clergy
do not have to wear a 'Geneva' gown or even a 'dog collar'. Not only
should the message be preached in the language best understood by
the congregation, but the terminology of theology should be expressed
the way common people can understand. Nevertheless, theological
meaning must not be sacrificed on the altar of comprehension. Instead
of employing terms that would water down the Gospel, the congre-
gations should be taught the original meaning of the term. One
instance is the mustard seed. This is a crop not found in America or
Africa. Instead of substituting a local grain for it, the term should be
employed and the explanation given. While the content of God's
word should remain what it is, the expression of it in teaching,
preaching, and singing should be made relevant. Drama and story-
telling, for instance, should be considered more seriously in Africa.
Any method that helps the advance of Christ's message should be
employed.

2 Religious syncretism

In a recent talk to church leaders in East Africa, the Rev. John R. W. Stott described syncretism as 'a fruit cocktail of religions.' Eric Sharpe defines it as 'any form of religion in which elements from more than one original religious tradition are combined.'

Christianity has gone full circle in Africa. In Africa, or in the Third World for that matter, Christianity has come to the stage it was at in the second century. Just as syncretism plagued the church in the days of the apologists, so it challenges the historic faith in Africa today. Donald McGavran's evaluation fits the situation in Africa today:

> It seems clear that during the next decades Christians again, as in the first two centuries, will fight the long battle against syncretism and religious relativism. And for the same reason – namely, that they are again in intimate contact with multitudes of non-Christian *peers* who believe that many paths lead to the top of the mountain. The concept of the cosmic Christ, some maintain, is a way out of the 'arrogance which stains the Christian when he proclaims Jesus Christ as the only Way to the Father'. Other Christians believe that the concept of a 'cosmic Christ operating through many religions' sacrifices truth, for if there are, in fact, many revelations, then each voices an approximation of the truth…. As hundreds of Christian and semi-Christian denominations spring into being across Africa, Asia, and other lands of earth, some will inevitably hold biblical and others syncretistic views of the Person of Christ.

Incentives for syncretism in Africa are not hard to find. The incentives for universalism (the idea that all will be saved in the end) are the same for syncretism, since only a thin line separates the two ideologies. The reasons for growing syncretistic tendencies in Africa may be summed up briefly.

(i) The prevailing wind of religious relativism in the older churches of the West is being carried abroad by the liberal missionaries in person and through literature.

(ii) The crying need for universal solidarity in the world fosters religious respect one for the other.

(iii) Political awareness in Africa carries with it a search for ideological identity. Some theologians seek to find this identity in African traditional religions.

(iv) Emotional concerns for the ancestors who died before the advent of Christianity force some theologians to call for recognition of the religious practices of pre-Christian idol worshippers.

(v) Cultural revolution promotes a return to the traditional socio-religio-cultural way of life in Africa. Since it is hard to separate culture from religion, the tendency is to make them identical and cling to idolatrous practices as being an authentic African way of life.

(vi) Inadequate biblical teaching has left the average Christian with an inability in 'rightly handling the Word of truth.' Syncretistic or neoorthodox teachers bring their views, and even Christian leaders fail to discern what is right according to the teaching of God's Word.

(vii) The African loves to get along with everybody. He is, therefore, not inclined to offend his neighbour by letting him know what the Bible says about non-Christian religions. That is why liberal ecumenism is thriving in Africa.

(viii) Liberal Christianity has done a thorough job in picking up key brains from the Third World and grooming them in liberal schools in the Western world.

(ix) The study of comparative religions, without affirmation of the uniqueness of Christianity, has helped produce theologians of syncretistic persuasion.

(x) The legitimate desire to make Christianity truly African has not been matched with the discernment not to tamper with the inspired inerrant content of the revealed Word of God.

The spirit of syncretism in Africa is predominant today both inside and outside church circles. Otto Stahlke accurately describes the contemporary situation when he writes, 'The syncretistic tendency, the attempt to blend and reconcile various religions, is not new, but never before has it been so prominently espoused by a leading agency for many Christian churches. Promotion of this point of view has come from philosophers, sociologists, anthropologists, comparative religionists, and some avant garde theologians.'

An African anthropologist, Okot p'Bitek says:

> In my view the student of African religions needs to soak himself thoroughly in the day-to-day life of the people whose thought-systems and beliefs he wishes to study.... When attending ceremonies, he must not stand apart as a spectator, but join in

fully, singing the songs, chanting the chants and dancing the dances.

P'Bitek calls for syncretism not only in matters of pagan religious festivities but also in pagan immoral practices. He considers the Christian teaching that sex be confined to marriage alone as being Western, and states that it must be rejected by the African. Realizing that Christian ethical teaching is based on God's Word, the university lecturer condemns the Apostle Paul in a derogatory manner:

> This ex-Pharisee who has been described as the ugly little Jew, was a small man barely five feet tall, bow-legged, a chronic malaria patient with serious eye trouble. We learn from Acts Chapter IX that he became a mental case for a short time, and on recovery he joined the Christians whom he had formerly persecuted. Paul was a great woman hater.

Since the 'Western world is still a prisoner of St. Paul's thwarted sexual morality' the African should outgrow that delusion and follow the type of morality which allows free sex. P'Bitek considers that African. He writes, 'In most African societies, having sexual intercourse with married women by persons other than their husbands is strictly forbidden; but unmarried women enjoy both unmarried and married men.' He suggests, 'It is important for African leaders to consider whether sexual ethics in their countries should be based on St. Paul's prejudices against women and sex, or built on the African viewpoint which takes sex as a good thing.'

In political circles, recognition of all religions as being good is ideal for national solidarity. Religious tolerance in almost all African countries is admirable. Christians should continue to pray for men in government that such a peaceful atmosphere may continue. But religious tolerance is quite different from enforced unity or regulated practice against one's religious convictions. The philosophy of authenticity in Zaire has resulted in enforced unity of all Protestant Christians into one Church of Christ in Zaire, which could lead to compromising syncretistic situations. But the worst situation is that reported in the Republic of Chad. According to reports, Christians are being forced to undergo initiation into pagan rites. Some Christian leaders have been imprisoned, churches burnt down, and missionaries expelled, because they rejected what would amount to syncretism.

It is rather sad that some Christian leaders are encouraging government interference in religious affairs, because they want to encourage
ecumenism. Thus Professor John Mbiti has written: 'Denominationa-
lism and its proliferation... are the product of human selfishness and
weakness. Our church leaders in Kenya, present and past, African and
expatriate, have made a mess of the church through inheriting and
agreeing to accept divisions, through multiplying divisions, and through
perpetuating divisions.' The Kenyan theologian therefore expresses a
wish that the Kenyan government would 'set up a ministry of religious
affairs' to straighten out this mess. Situations similar to that of Zaire
may not be far away in other African countries. When such things take
place, syncretistic practices of some semi-Christian groups will likely
pervade a wider Christian spectrum.

Apart from secular writing and government encouragement for
syncretism, the study of comparative religions is another major factor.
Many of the universities in Black Africa have departments of religions.
The primary goal of these departments, far from being the spiritual
growth of individual Christian students, is academic excellence. The
tendency is to study Christianity, Islam, and African traditional religions
in a detached manner. The journal of the department of religious
studies at the University of Ibadan best illustrates this. The journal is
called *Orita*, a Yoruba word meaning a junction. The design on the
cover shows three roads meeting in the centre. One road is labelled
Islam, one is labelled African traditional religion, and one is labelled
Christianity. The head of the department is a Christian, but the editor
of the journal is a Muslim. One explanation of this mixed arrangement
would be that the department seeks only to understand the encounter
of these three religions in Africa. An evident fact is that the journal
presupposes the validity of all these religions, and is silent on the
uniqueness of the Christian faith. Thus the seeds of syncretism, and
the implication of universalism, are planted in the minds of theological
students, many of whom become religious teachers in schools and
colleges. Some find their way to the pulpit. Admittedly, some will
survive the test and grow stronger, but not a few will end up proclaiming
a syncretistic message.

The teaching of African traditional religions in secondary schools is
becoming increasingly popular. It is being suggested in some circles
that religious knowledge teachers should present just the objective
facts of Islam, African traditional religions, and Christianity, without
showing what they believe. The young teenagers should then be left to
sort out for themselves what to believe. But since there are some good

elements in every religion, would it not be easier for an immature student to pick up the good points of each and make up a new religion? This may fulfil the aspirations of some theologians that Africa should come up with a religion that is modern and truly African. As a matter of fact, Dr. J. K. Agbeti of Ghana feels that the survival of Christianity in Africa lies with the traditional religions rather than with the prophetic Word of God. He writes, 'The true theological interpretation of the traditional African religious experience could be a strong springboard from which the tottering Christianity of Africa today may be rescued and rooted more meaningfully in the African soil.' Evidently this is a call for a syncretistic form of Christianity.

Some church leaders today frown upon the missionaries for declaring the unique Lordship of Christ as presented in the Scriptures. Criticizing the earlier presentation in Africa of the unique Christ, who would not share room with idols, Joachim Getonga writes, 'To be regarded as a true Christian in those days, a person had to abandon almost all the culture which he had acquired from his own African society. He had to detach himself from virtually all the beliefs of his parents, throw away his native clothes and put on Western dress or ornaments in order to be accepted into the Christian faith. Tribal dances in particular were considered diabolical.' Getonga then appeals to all Christian preachers to 'rethink the place of their cultural heritage and to reconstruct what was destroyed during those pioneering days of evangelization.' One is tempted to ask Getonga what native clothes he has in mind and whether he would honestly like to go back to them? What concerns us here is the question of 'the beliefs of his parents.' African Christians who have found it necessary to burn every idol have followed precedents set in the Scriptures (Acts 19). Christianity stands to judge every culture, destroying elements that are incompatible with the Word of God, employing compatible modes of expression for its advance, and bringing new life to its adherents, the qualitative life that begins at the moment of conversion and culminates eternally with the imminent return of our Lord Jesus Christ.

Even some of the most outstanding theologians in Africa have not avoided universalistic tendencies. Professor John Mbiti holds that all men will be saved in the final analysis. He affirms, 'There is not a single soul, however debased or even unrepentant, which can successfully "flee" from the Spirit of God (Psalm 139:1–18). God's patient waiting for the soul's repentance must in the end be surely more potent than the soul's reluctance to repent and turn to him (2 Peter 3:9). The harmony of the heavenly worship would be impaired if, out of the one hundred in the sheepfold, there is one soul which continues to languish in Sheol or "the lake of fire".'

Professor Bolaji Idowu objects to localizing theology. He would also eschew syncretism. But one wonders where his high view of African traditional religions is leading. He writes, 'To call African traditional religion "idolatry" is to be grossly unfair to its essence.' But if pagan gods are not idols, then what are they? Idowu claims with the adherents that these gods are ministers of the Almighty God. To recognize the reality of these man-made gods is to reject the scriptural view of these 'dumb idols' (Isaiah 2:8; 40:18–20; 41:7; 1 Thessalonians 1:9; 1 Corinthians 8:4–6). While it is true that the pagan is conscious of the existence of a Supreme Being through general revelation, his vision of the Supreme Being is distorted because of original sin. The image of God in man, though not obliterated, is disfigured to the point that he is considered dead in 'trespasses and sins' (Ephesians 2:1), until he receives new life in Christ. His worship of creatures rather than the Creator can be described adequately only as idolatry. What Africa needs is the unadulterated Gospel of Jesus Christ who declares authoritatively and finally, 'I am the Way, the Truth, and the Life. No man cometh unto the Father but by me' (John 14:6).

Conclusion

Syncretism will increasingly become popular in the Third World. The watered down concept of 'Salvation Today' hatched at Bangkok in 1972–73 will give impetus to syncretistic and universalistic yearnings in the Third World. The persistent urge for cultural revolution in Africa will energize the forces of syncretism. The days of persecution for the Bible-believing Christian may not be too far away. Christians all over the world should pray for grace for the Third World followers and heralds of the unique Christ. Meanwhile, the Bible-believing Christian should respect and pray 'for kings and all who are in high positions, that we may lead a quiet and peaceful life, godly and respectful in every way' (1 Timothy 2:2). Christians in Africa should realize that to stand for the uniqueness of Christ will not be popular as ungodliness increases in the world. There may come a time when Christians will have to say, 'For we cannot but speak the things which we have seen and heard' (Acts 4:20). They may even have to say, 'We ought to obey God rather than men' (Acts 5:29) and face the consequences that Stephen and others after him have faced.

We may conclude with this appropriate observation from Dr. Donald McGavran about Christianity:

> It purges all cultures – Christian, partially Christian, and non-Christian alike. Since it purges twentieth-century Christianity in a way it did not purge seventeenth-century Christianity, it also purges twentieth-century Bantu religion and Marxist religion as their adherents come to believe on Jesus Christ.

The final challenge for the African Christian is to make Christianity culturally relevant while holding fast to its ever-abiding message.

4

CHRISTIANITY AS AN AFRICAN RELIGION

(April 1975)

When I was in Malawi recently, I was told of the leader of a religious sect which promotes traditional ancestor worship. This leader lifted up the Koran and asked, 'Whose book is this?' His listeners replied, 'The Arabs' book.' He went on, 'Whose religion is Islam?' The reply was, 'It is the religion of the Arabs.' He did the same thing with Christianity. The conclusion drawn was that Christianity is the white man's religion. The audience was invited to reject both religions as being foreign. Ancestor worship was then declared the religion of the Africans.

In these challenging days there are many voices being heard which claim that Christianity is an alien religion, in which the African should have no hand. Is this a valid claim? It is my conviction that, to the contrary, Christianity is truly an African religion. Let me explain why.

1 African traditional religions

The various ethnic African groups have their traditional religions as an answer to the reality of their existence. The primary question being raised today is that of the nature of these religions in relation to Christianity. The Apostle Paul categorically points out that the worship of pagan gods is a distortion of God's revelation in nature (Romans 1:18–23). Whatever rationalization we may try to make, the worship of gods in Africa is idolatry. This is not a denial of the universality of general revelation. God truly has not left Himself without a witness. His goodness to people irrespective of whether they are good or evil is evidence of His witness to all people (Acts 14:17). His marvellous work of creation is a further pointer to His supreme power (Psalm 19). But the revelation has been distorted through the disobedience of the very first commandment. Man has not adhered to the one true God and to Him alone, as he was commanded to do (Exodus 20:3; Deuteronomy 6:4); rather he has set up his own gods.

The depravity evident in African traditional religions is evident among all peoples of the earth. The Psalmist declares, 'The Lord looks down from heaven upon the children of men, to see if there are any that act wisely, that seek after God. They have all gone astray, they are all alike corrupt; there is none that does good, no not one' (Psalm 14:2,3). Paul echoes this in the New Testament (Romans 3:10–18). The worship of idolatry is as old as man from the Fall. Adam's effort to clothe himself instead of being clothed with God's righteousness was the beginning of that search for answers away from God. The Philistines, the Babylonians, the Greeks, and the Romans, all indulged in idolatry. No people are excluded. The Arabs used to worship many 'Jinns' (spirits). Stonehenge in southern England is a living evidence of Druidism, which was the heathen worship of the early inhabitants of the United Kingdom. Human sacrifice was a part of Druid worship and was only abolished in Roman days.

While pagan worship was a part of the religion of these respective peoples, they could change to other religions of their choice. Most Arabs accepted Islam and became Muslims. Islam is now associated with Arabs as their religion. Thanks to the faithful witness of Christian missionaries, the British people no longer claim Druidism as their religion. They are now Christians, and Christianity is legitimately recognized as the British religion. Why should this not be the case in Africa, where at least one-third of all Africans are adherents of the Christian religion in one form or another? Why are there voices still denying the fact that Christianity is an African religion, when more than 150 million people of Africa call themselves Christian? To these adherents of the Christian faith at least, Christianity is an African religion. They are Africans and Christianity is their religion.

2 Historical Relationship of Christianity and Africa

Although in modern times missionaries from Europe and North America brought the gospel to Africa, they are not the first representatives of Christianity on our continent. As a matter of fact, history shows that Christianity's ties are closer with Africa than with Europe or North America.

God's call to man for revealing His will to mankind first came to an

Asian, Abraham. It was through his descendants, the Jews, that God gave the message of salvation. But this does not give Jews any monopoly on the gospel. Nor does this make their culture in any way superior to other cultures. God was merely using them to fulfil His purpose for the redemption of the world. Jesus was born, brought up, died and rose again in Asia, and not in any European country. I am not aware of any evidence that any of the writers of the books of the Bible were European. Jesus Christ, the founder of Christianity, never walked in Europe. As a matter of fact, Christianity did not reach Europe until about 20 years after Christ's death and resurrection, when Lydia became the first European convert through the work of Paul (Acts 16:15).

In contrast to this, the Bible presents many historical facts on the relationship of Africa with the land of the Bible, Palestine. In the Old Testament, it was out of their bondage in Africa that God redeemed His people. Egypt is a part of Africa. The Queen of Sheba who visited Solomon was from Ethiopia in Africa, according to tradition. Moses, the head of the Israeli nation, was married to a girl who was possibly an African (Numbers 12:1). It was an African who rescued Jeremiah from a pit when no one else would do it (Jeremiah 38:7). It was prophesied long ago that God's work would some day have tremendous impact in Africa. Egypt and Ethiopia were spoken of representatively: 'Envoys will come out of Egypt; Ethiopia will quickly stretch out her hands to God' (Psalm 68:31).

The New Testament, too, presents the direct link of Africa with the Holy Land. In fulfilment of a prophecy made seven hundred years earlier, Jesus Christ was brought to Africa as a baby for safety from wicked King Herod. God said, 'I called my son out of Egypt' (Matthew 2:15). So the Saviour born in Asia, walked the soil of Africa. When Jesus was carrying His cross to the hill for crucifixion, He was unable to continue much longer. It was an African who carried the cross the rest of the way. On the day of Pentecost, Africa was represented. Settlers of Cyrene in North Africa were there when the Holy Spirit inaugurated the Christian church (Acts 2:10). An African from Ethiopia was one of the first converts outside native Jewish circles (Acts 8). When the first missionary conference was held, an African was there. Mentioned among the faithful disciples in Antioch was Simeon, nicknamed Niger (Acts 13:1). Niger, from which the river Niger and the countries of Niger and Nigeria are named, means black.

During the earliest period of Christianity, North Africa and Asia

Minor were the two areas with the strongest churches. Africa in the first four centuries of our era produced outstanding theologians. Augustine of Hippo has had more lasting influence on Christian theology than any other person since the Apostle Paul. His African practical mind can still be noted in both Roman Catholic and Protestant theologies. Cyprian, Athanasius, Tertullian, and Origen were all outstanding African theologians. It was due to internal squabbles and lack of vision that Christianity then spread northward to western Europe and the British Isles. Converted Europe then later brought Christianity to Black Africa. One may see the cycle of the spread of Christianity to Asia, Africa, Europe, America, and back to Africa, and the rest of the world. Perhaps the cycle will repeat itself before long, when Africans and Asians will again take the gospel to Europe. Church attendance in Germany today is 2%, England 4%, and Kenya 40%. To claim that Christianity is a white man's religion only because white missionaries brought the gospel two hundred years ago is not historically accurate. But this does not give an Asian or an African any monopoly on Christianity. God gave His revelation to the whole world. The invitation comes to all people of all cultures: 'Turn to me, and be saved, all the ends of the earth; for I am God, and there is no other' (Isaiah 45:22). 'Come to me, all you who are weary and burdened, and I will give you rest' (Matthew 11:28).

If anyone wants to reject Christianity, he must do so on other grounds and not on the excuse that it is a white man's religion. We are indebted to modern missionaries for bringing the gospel to Africa, but they are only messengers. They would fully identify themselves with the declarations of John the Baptist and of Paul: 'He must increase but I must decrease' (John 3:30); 'Let God be true, and every man a liar' (Romans 3:4). Africans have a right to change their religion from heathen worship to Christianity. Having done so, Christianity can become an African religion. In fact, historically that is what has happened. Historically Christianity was thriving in Africa long before it reached the British Isles and North America, from where so many of the Protestant missionaries came. We can, therefore, rightly call Christianity an African religion.

3 The Nature of Christianity

Particularism and universalism are paradoxically both features of Christianity. Christianity is both exclusive and inclusive. It is particularistic right from its inception. When mankind lapsed into idolatry and all forms of godlessness, it pleased God to call a particular man, Abraham, to reveal His will for mankind through him (Genesis 12:1–3). Through a particular line, Abraham's descendants, His message of redemption would reach all mankind. Through Abraham all mankind would be blessed. It is not bigotry nor is it nationalism or racism to speak of the God of Israel. Israel from time to time has become introspective and arrogant, thus failing in its mission to the world. Nevertheless, it was chosen by God to convey the message of salvation to the whole world.

Universalism in the sense of God's revelation for the redemption of all mankind, is just as much a part of God's revelation as particularism in God's choice of Israel as a nation. Israel was to be a light to the Gentiles. The God of Israel extends His invitation to all people: 'Turn to me and be saved, all the ends of the earth. For I am God, and there is no other. By myself I have sworn, from my mouth has gone forth in righteousness a word that shall not return to me. Every knee shall bow, every tongue shall swear' (Isaiah 45:22, 23). In the New Testament the gospel writers interpret Christ's life and message in terms of His benefits to the world. He is the bread and water of life for whoever would come. God's love and provision is for the whole world (John 3:16), and this includes the African. Jesus Christ, the centre of Christianity, is for the African.

In the rest of the New Testament, the universal nature of Christianity becomes evident both in doctrine and practice. On the day of Pentecost Asians, Africans and Europeans were all there (Acts 2:9–11). They can all claim Christianity as their religion. In describing the composition of the Church as the body of Christ, Paul sees all men as members of that one body (1 Corinthians 12:13). In that body 'there is neither Jew nor Greek, there is neither slave nor free, there is neither male nor female, for you are all one in Christ Jesus' (Galatians 3:28). No one racial class or sex group has a monopoly on the claims of Christ's Church. Christianity is an African religion to its African adherents, just as it is European to the European, American to the American, or Asian to the Asian followers of Christ.

4 The Practice of Christianity

Since Christianity is truly an African religion, Africans should be made to feel it so. What remains to be done is to help African Christians feel very much at home in the Church. Christian doctrine should be expressed in terms that Africans can understand. Practices that enhance the growth of the Church, the maturity and enjoyment of the African believer, should be promoted. Take for instance the formal prayers written in the 18th century. Both the language and concepts are not easy for today's British youth to understand, let alone African youth. Should not African clergymen revise them and recast them in language and concepts easily understood by the African youths? Perhaps greater involvement by the congregation in a church service would appeal more to the Africans. This should be explored. Clothing and musical instruments are also to be considered. Whatever would reflect the glory of Christ in His Church in Africa, and make the African feel that 'this is *my* faith', should be promoted. If there are any alien beliefs or practices mingled with Christianity, the answer is not to throw away the baby with the bathwater. Rather, we should purge biblical faith in Africa of those alien features and express the unchanging biblical faith in Africa for the Africans, since it is as much an African religion as it is a European religion. What we need in today's Africa is not a return to the old traditional religions, or even a borrowing of some of the pagan practices to add to Christianity. Our greatest need is to live up to the claims we make as Christians in Africa, and promote the Christian message for Africa in all areas of life and everywhere possible as true ambassadors of Christ.

Recommendations

In conclusion, let me make the following recommendations.

a. Know the truth and defend it, with all at your disposal, including your life's blood. Our Lord appeals to us 'to contend for the faith which was once for all delivered to the saints' (Jude 3). The way ahead may not be easy. Jesus never promised us an easy road. Jesus says, 'If any man would come after me, let him deny himself and take up his cross and follow me' (Mark 8:34). The Word of God further says, 'For it has been granted to you that for the sake of Christ you should not only believe in Him but also suffer for His sake' (Philippians 1:29).

b. Discern the voices. Get your marching orders from the Word of God and not from men's voices, be they from within or without the camp. 'Beloved, do not believe every spirit, but test the spirits to see whether they are of God; for many false prophets have gone out into the world' (1 John 4:1).

c. Reject moratorium but promote self-reliance. Some advocates of moratorium today see the work of missionaries as a part of the system of colonial servitude. While we do agree that there have been failures on the part of some missionaires to live up to the gospel of Christ, yet we cannot deny the fact that they came as truly the messengers of good tidings. The One who sent them said, 'If the Son shall make you free, you will be free indeed' (John 8:36). We should, therefore, be thankful to God and His messengers. The rejection of moratorium, however, should not mean that our churches should now maintain a servile, begging attitude. Our priority should be to promote the training of nationals, with missionaries helping as necessary, so that both black and white will move together as workers with Christ (2 Corinthians 6:1).

d. Evangelize or perish. It would take a church only two or three generations to go out of existence if it does not evangelize. The youngest Christian in our churches in Africa today is not likely to be around in another hundred years. The thing to bear in mind is that if Jesus Christ should come today, millions of people would go to a Christless eternity. This should motivate every Christian in Africa to say, 'Woe to me if I do not preach the gospel' (1 Corinthians 9:16).

e. Contextualize without compromise. Let Christianity truly find its home in Africa, by adopting local hymnology, using native language, idiom and concepts to express the unchanging faith. But always let our primary goal be that Jesus Christ might have the foremost place. 'So whether you eat or drink, or whatever you do, do all to the glory of God' (1 Corinthians 10:31).

f. Pray for and be prepared for revival. While we should all be thankful for the revivals of the past, such as the East African Revival, dare we dwell on the blessings of the past? While we should rejoice over the victory of the gospel through the missionaries of the past, and through the earlier generation of African Christians, should we not plead with the Lord to provide us with more Joshuas and Timothys for today and tomorrow? God has promised, 'Behold I will do a new thing' (Isaiah 43:19). May it happen in our day, even if it means some changes in our image and our value structures.

g. Become more missionary-minded. Look beyond the borders of your country and further afield, to the pagan strongholds of our continent, and to the western world trapped in materialistic attractions. The world is the field. The church in Africa and elsewhere is the only agent for sowing the seed (Matthew 13:38; Acts 1:8). May the Lord help the members of His Body, the Church, as we lift up His banner of victory in Africa in particular and the world in general.

5

THEOLOGICAL ISSUES IN AFRICA

(September 1975)

The political, economic, and social changes that have swept in a spectacular way through Africa in recent years have affected people's mentality. A search for identity has become a leading factor in African life, and not least in African religious life. For here, too, the winds of change have been at work. Growth of the Christian community has been phenomenal. New patterns of church relationships have emerged. Africans have come into the leadership roles. New movements have arisen. Influences from abroad continue to make their mark. All these factors have contributed to a search for ecclesiastical and theological identity in contemporary Africa. Among the key issues which revolve around this quest we may identify: the African cultural revolution, African theology, the ecumenical movement, and black theology.

1 African Cultural Revolution

It is estimated that between eight hundred and a thousand ethnic groups exist in Africa. Admittedly, certain characteristics may distinguish Africans from non-Africans, such as the former's practical approach to problems, solving problems more often by compromise than by conflict, and the emphasis on communal life as a family or tribe. But in addition, major differences exist between Africans themselves, such as in language, taboos, marriage patterns, and religions. It is, therefore, difficult to speak of 'African culture' as such. Nevertheless, there are enough similarities to warrant this homogeneous description.

Ironically, the call for a return to African culture does not come so much from the rural dwellers who are still very much African, but from the sophisticated urban dwellers, such as government officials and church leaders. Perhaps one reason why this interest stems from the higher class is the fact that these are the people who have become more aware of the need for African personality. They have come face to face with colonial strictures. While the illiterate rural African is seeking to have a taste of the fruit of technology, the sophisticated urban African has come to discover that there is more to life than material pleasure. Cultural background as the basic source of one's personality becomes most desirable. Hence the call for authenticity.

The emphasis on cultural revolution is a general trend throughout Africa. In Kenya a team of traditional dancers is maintained to perform during official functions. In Ivory Coast and Benin the question of initiation and other pagan rites is becoming a dilemma for churches in certain areas. In Swaziland the king's daughters appear topless on the national currency notes, as a part of that nation's cultural renaissance. And Nigeria plans to host the Festival of Black and African Arts and Culture shortly.

The call for authenticity in Zaire, which began with a change from western and biblical names to authentic Zairean names, has advanced beyond that stage. Pagan initiation has now been introduced in the schools. A Zairean Christian leader has hailed this as 'a sign of revival for the church of Christ.'[1] Christian theological studies have been drastically curtailed. It is reported that Christian religious instruction in the schools has been replaced by political indoctrination. Some church leaders claim that they are Zaireans first and Christians secondly.

In the Republic of Chad cultural revolution has led to the loss of human lives. The government of the late president Ngarta Tombalbaye saw in pagan initiation a practice worthy of cultural revival. In the ancient practice of initiation in Chad, the young candidate is supposed to renounce all his past experiences of any kind and go through a stage of new birth as he is brought into supposed contact with the ancestors during a period of isolation from public life lasting about three months. Committed Chadian Christians refused to undergo the pagan practices and some were tortured to death.

The search for authenticity through culture remains a desirable element in many African societies. The attitude of Christians toward cultural renaissance need not be negative. Culture as a way of life must be maintained. Jesus Christ became a man in order to save men. In becoming incarnate, he was involved in the Jewish culture – wearing their clothes, eating their food, thinking in their thought patterns. But while He went through all that, He was without sin, addressing both Jewish and Gentile people authoritatively as the Son of God. Jesus would not have come to make Africans become American Christians nor to cause Europeans to become Indian Christians. It is God's will that Africans, on accepting Christ as their Saviour, become Christian Africans. Africans who become Christians should, therefore, remain Africans wherever their culture does not conflict with the Bible. It is the Bible that must judge the culture. Where a conflict results, the cultural element must give away.[2]

2 African Theology

Christian theology needs to address itself specifically to the African situation. African theologians of the first four centuries of Christianity made a vital contribution to the development of theology in the universal Church. Those early African theologians include Origen, Athanasius, Tertullian, and Augustine. African theologians today should also make their own contribution to theology for the benefit of the Church universal. If this is what is meant by African theology, then it is a noble effort worthy of support.

Unfortunately, many theologians spend their time defending African traditional religions and practices that are incompatible with biblical teaching. Some writers have recently sought to justify pagan initiation rites. Speaking in support of initiation, Bongeye Senza Masa of the All Africa Conference of Churches welcomes 'the decision to turn the school into a centre of traditional initiation, where ancestral values are integrated into the modern educational system'.[3] Many Christians in Chad have laid down their lives for their objection to initiation rites. I visited Chad and received confirmation from many Chadian Christians that these rites are pagan practices. Yet some African Christian leaders are defending the practice. The burning desire to defend African personality is given precedence over scriptural injunction.

Theology in Africa is increasingly turning to African traditional religions rather than to the Bible as its absolute source. Agbeti of Ghana writes, 'When we talk about "African Theology" we should mean the interpretation of the pre-Christian and pre-Moslem African people's experience of their God.'[4] He speaks of African theology as 'a theology which will critically systematize the traditional African experience of God'.[5] It seems that Agbeti is advocating a return to African traditional religions rather than expressing Christianity more meaningfully to the African. Other advocates of African theology do not go so far as Agbeti. Various theologians give their interpretations of what African theology means. Mbiti, who has done extensive original work in this area, has said, 'It is all too easy to use the phrase "African Theology"; but to state what that means, or even to show its real nature, is an entirely different issue.'[6]

One thing, however, seems certain concerning most of the advocates of African theology. Turner sums it up well:

> It does not seem to help much to speak of 'African Theology'. The term is viewed with suspicion because the interest in traditional religion associated with it calls up in the minds of many a return to paganism. The phrase 'an African Theology' has about it, therefore, the quality of a slogan of vindication. It refers first to the attempt to find points of similarity between Christian notions and those drawn from the traditional religions of Africa. Second, it refers to the hope that a systematic theology expressed in the language and concepts of traditional religion and culture, may one day be written.... The phrase implies in its popular usage an attempt to amalgamate elements of Christian and elements of traditional belief.[7]

African theology seems to be heading for syncretism and universalism. This subject I have discussed at length elsewhere.[8] Suffice it here to sound a note of warning that the search for an African personality should not lead Africans to a compromising position. This is not to suggest a moratorium on further research on African thought patterns. But in the African evangelical effort to express Christianity in the context of Africa, the Bible must remain the absolute source. The Bible is God's written Word addressed to Africans — and to all peoples – within their cultural background.

The term 'African theology' has come to mean different things to different people. Furthermore, it has the inherent danger of syncretism. The term, therefore, is viewed with suspicion. It is more appropriate to talk of Christian theology, and then to define whatever context it is related to, e.g., reflections from Africa; the context of marriage in Africa; the spirit world in Africa. A continuing effort should be made to relate Christian theology to the changing situations in Africa, but only as the Bible is taken as the absolute Word of God can it have an authoritative and relevant message for Africa.

3 Ecumenical Theology

In Africa at least five leading concepts are included in ecumenical theology. Let me mention each in turn.

a. The Bible is becoming relative rather than normative. Among proponents of ecumenism other documents and experiences are becoming just as important as the Bible. Much of the emphasis on contextual theology is making human experiences normative. The conference of the World Council of Churches held in Bangkok in 1973 had as its theme 'Salvation Today'. Conference participants were encouraged to attend Buddhist temples and to participate in other religious functions in order to discover what these experiences may say about salvation.

b. Salvation is interpreted in terms of political, economic, and social liberation. The fifth General Assembly of the World Council of Churches met in Nairobi in 1975 under the general theme 'Jesus Christ Frees and Unites'. One of the published documents of the Assembly includes the following statement: 'We see the struggles for economic justice, political freedom, and cultural renewal as elements in the total liberation of the world through the mission of God…. This comprehensive notion of salvation demands of the whole of the people of God a matching comprehensive approach to their participation in salvation.'[9]

c. The Kingdom of God means a search for common humanity irrespective of religion. The old liberal concept of anonymous Christianity is now being revived in the African ecumenical movement. It is held that even non-Christians are already Christians without realizing it. The task of Christian missions is simply to make non-Christians aware of their salvation. The World Council Assembly at Nairobi included in its pre-Assembly publications an appeal for willingness 'to recognize the possibility of salvation among men of other religions and their religions themselves as possible means of salvation *for them*, because that is all they have until they are actually confronted with Christianity…. They may have been granted ultimate salvation by the grace of God, but they do not yet know Christ Jesus the Lord…. He is in them but they are not yet in Him…. When grace visits a Brahmin, a Buddhist, or a Muslim reading his scriptures, it is Christ alone who is received as light.'[10]

d. Dialogue rather than declaration is the approach to evangelism. To the minds of many ecumenicals, it is the height of arrogance to declare to men of other religions that Jesus is the only way to salvation. Many evangelicals see dialogue as a tool for better understanding of other religions, which will enhance an effective proclamation of the gospel. But to many liberal ecumenicals, dialogue is a part of the greater effort that should lead to more peaceful coexistence among peoples. Dialogue may lead to the fulfilment of the ecumenical utopian vision. It also presupposes Christ's presence in all religions. It is interesting to note that Hindus, Buddhists, and Muslims contributed to the production of the materials that were studied at Nairobi. At the Christian-Muslim dialogue at Broumana in 1972, the following declaration was made:

> Those who are christian (not Christians only) and those who are muslim (not Muslim only) are already together, in the sense that they are united not only in their friendship of God but also in their common commitment against false absolutes of our age and against the injustices these engender in the lives of men.[11]

A number of consultations have been held, in Hong Kong, Ghana, Senegal, and other places, to discuss dialogue. In many cases, worshipping together in different shrines and temples or churches is a part of or even a prerequisite for dialogue. 'Praying together, then, seems to be the beginning and the basis of dialogue.'[12]

e. A moratorium on missions is part of the liberation process. Ecumenical leaders use self-reliance to justify their call for a cessation of mission activites flowing from the West to the Third World. But their pronouncements have shown that the call for a moratorium goes deeper than this. Biblically-based Christian mission is seen as an oppressive measure from which people in the Third World ought to be redeemed. The Barbados Declaration, an ecumenical statement in 1971 respecting the situation in Latin America, categorically states, 'We conclude that the suspension of all missionary activity is the most appropriate policy for the good of Indian society and for the moral integrity of the churches involved.'[13]

Self-assertion is human, and anthropocentric theology, such as is promoted in ecumenism, fits this innate desire. One may expect the influence of ecumenical theology, therefore, to spread in Africa, since it makes human experience the basic source of theologizing. Evangelicals, for their part, must learn to move beyond the divinely revealed source to the human dimension where the action is. Holding the Bible as their basic source for Christian theology, they must discover how best to relate to the human situation in all areas, including the socio-politico-economic arena. Unless evangelicals delve more deeply into these human levels, they will find it difficult to gain a hearing in Africa today.

4 Black Theology

Black theology, which became evident among blacks of the United States in the 1960s, seeks to emphasize black consciousness and thereby to discover the dignity of the black man. Black consciousness does not necessarily refer to the pigmentation of the skin. Rather it means an awareness that the particular class of people called 'black' have been oppressed. Malcolm McVeigh of Nairobi University accurately sums up when he says: 'The primary concern of black theology is liberation, and one sees considerable attention devoted to defining the implications of Jesus' gospel for the downtrodden in the face of entrenched political, social and economic injustice.'[14]

That black theology was born in the United States and is now rooted in Southern Africa is no accident. As an ideology seeking to liberate the oppressed, that oppression becomes the root cause. Enslavement of Africans by whites is among the worst evils done by one class of people to another. It may be surpassed only by Hitler's massacre of six million Jews. Until about twenty years ago, American blacks experienced many kinds of humiliation on account of their race. The 270 thousand whites of Rhodesia have tried to dominate the 5.8 million Africans of that land, on the assumption that they are preserving Christian civilization. In apartheid South Africa today, the Soweto black dweller works to provide comfort for the white suburban inhabitants of ultramodern Johannesburg, but he benefits very little from the fruit of his labour. To keep the black man in perpetual bondage, the racist regime is reported to spend about $750 a year for the education of an average white child and only $45 for a black child.[15]

While I do not agree with the proponents of black theology for reasons to be given later, I fully identify myself with their condemnation of injustice. The search for human dignity is a scriptural principle. Jesus Christ so values human life that He became incarnate. Not one hair from anyone's head falls to the ground without God's knowledge and concern (Matthew 10:30). Thank God not all white people have been guilty of dehumanization. In fact, many white people have faced ridicule and even death for the sake of the black man. Therefore, generalization should be avoided in discussing this subject.

Furthermore, Christianity should be judged by what its Founder has said in His Word rather than by what professing followers have done or not done. The Bible is God's Word. Even if all men become liars and unfaithful, God remains faithful (2 Timothy 2:13). Christians may fail and have failed, but biblical Christianity has not failed because Jesus never fails. Black theology, though raising the right questions, has been carried away by emotions. Many black theology leaders have cast aside the Bible or stripped it of its absolute authority. The humanistic ethical principle that the end justifies the means has become the marching orders for liberation enthusiasts. That is why some theologians go so far as to justify violence on the basis of Christian revelation. A closer look at the nature of black theology shows that the system, as propounded by many of its exponents, is incompatible with biblical Christianity.

a. Black theology is reactionary. Steve Biko of South Africa gave the motif of black theology in Hegelian terminology: 'The *thesis* is in fact a strong white racism and therefore, the *antithesis* to this must *ipso facto* be a strong solidarity amongst the blacks on whom this white racism seeks to prey. Out of these two situations we can therefore hope to reach some kind of balance – a true humanity where power politics will have no place.'[16] According to this thesis, all white people, regardless of their relationship to Jesus Christ, are oppressors. Biko described them as 'irresponsible people from Coca Cola and hamburger cultural backgrounds.'[17] Black people, whether Christians or non-Christians, 'must sit as one big unit, and no fragmentation and distraction from the mainstream of events [can] be allowed'[18] in opposing the whites. A synthesis, or peaceful coexistence, may then result from this conflict.

This approach may fit Hegelian-Marxist theory, but it is not in keeping with the spirit of Jesus Christ. As the salt of the earth (Matthew 5:13), Christians should know no race barriers. Tertullian, an African theologian of the third century, spoke in the vein of New Testament Christianity when he declared, 'Christians are members of the third race.' Just as it is wrong for any Christian to support racial prejudice and oppression, so it is wrong for black Christians to lump all whites into one category and condemn them all. Rather than pitting thesis against antithesis on the basis of race, Christians from belligerent camps should stand as the synthesis, with Jesus Christ as the Head of the newly created body, the Church (Ephesians 4:15).

b. Black theology is relativistic and situational. For the Christian, the Bible is the absolute authority on which to base all theological and ethical formulations. Black theology, however, sets up human experience as the basic term of reference. Basil Moore writes, 'Black Theology is a situational theology. And the situation is that of the black man in South Africa.'[19] Biko, in rejecting absolutes, writes of black theology, 'It grapples with existential problems and does not claim to be a theology of absolutes.'[20] A popular motto found on many public vehicles in Nigeria is: 'No condition is permanent.' This is an apt description of the human condition. Man comes and goes. Human struggles constantly shift. Empires rise and fall. A theology that bases itself on human experience, rather than seeking answers for human experience from the absolute Word of God is as helpful as a sailboat without sails. Situation ethics, which allows immorality if love dictates the situation, must be firmly rejected as being out of line with the absolute teaching of the Scriptures. Bible-believing Christians should reject black theology on the same basis. The absolute Word of God must be the measuring rod of the varying, fleeting situations.

c. Black theology is characterized by humanism. It is true that salvation history has man as God's object of love and care. 'What is man that Thou dost take thought of him? And the son of man, that Thou dost care for him? Yet Thou has made him a little lower than God, and dost crown him with glory and majesty' (Psalm 8:4–5). But it is equally true that the Word of God has the final word on man's nature. The Bible speaks of the dignity of man, God's appointed ruler of His creation (Genesis 2:28). The same Word describes man's distorted, dissipating nature following the Fall (Genesis 3; Romans 1). Black theology, on the other hand, sees only man's dignity. 'It begins with people – specific people, in a specific situation, and with specific problems to face.'[21] A theology that begins with man will end there, missing the One who has spoken (Hebrews 1:1, 2).

The Bible is called on to conform to what black theology has said about man. Mpunzi states, 'Black theology has no room for the traditional Christian pessimistic view of man, the view that we are all by nature overwhelmingly and sinfully selfish.... This pessimism about man is therefore an ally in our own undermining of ourselves.'[22] Human dignity, in the sense that man is the master of his own fate, is the position advocated by radical proponents of black theology. The logical outcome of humanism is a replacement of God with man. That is what black theology seems to be doing.

d. Black theology dethrones the Omnipotent God and enthrones man. The gospel is described as 'black power'. James Cone of Union Theological Seminary in New York declares, 'Black Theology puts black identity in a theological context, showing that black power is not only consistent with the gospel of Jesus Christ, but that it *is* the gospel of Jesus Christ.'[23] If black power, which is described as the secular term for black theology,[24] is the gospel, it is appropriate then to find out what this gospel has to say about God. Basil Moore attempts to strip God bare of all absolute attributes derived from the pages of the Scriptures through centuries of biblical studies. He argues:

> Concepts such as omnipotence and omniscience ring fearfully of the immovable, military-backed South African government and its Special Branch. These, however, are the images learned from Western Theology, and their biblical justification is dubious. Black Theology cannot afford to have any truck with these images which lend religious support to a fascist type of authoritarianism. Nor should it lend ear to the pious clap-trap which asserts that man cannot be free, he can only choose whose slave he will be – Christ's or the state's.[25]

Moore describes the god of black theology, made in the image of the oppressed who are crying for liberation:

> Thus Black Theology needs to explore images of God which are not sickening reflections of the white man's power-made authoritarianism…. God is no authoritarian king issuing commandments and rewarding or punishing according to our obedience or disobedience. Rather, God is discovered and known in the search for and experience of liberation, which is the wholeness of human life found only in the unity of liberating, life-affirming and dignifying relationships…. An appropriate symbol of this understanding of God would be that 'God is Freedom'.[26]

Satan's attempt to usurp God's throne ended in utter failure. Throughout the ages he has also energized man to try to dethrone God. The fact that a racist regime has abused power is no reason for man to deprive God, his Creator, of His rightful kingship. The Almighty

God, Father of the Lord Jesus Christ, has authoritatively declared, 'I am God and there is no other; I am God, and there is no one like me' (Isaiah 46:9). The highest human dignity a person can bring to his fellow Africans or anyone else is to invite them to bow to the Lordship of Christ and the Father, joining all other loyal creatures in singing, 'Amen. Blessing and glory and wisdom and thanksgiving and honour and power and might be unto our God for ever and ever. Amen' (Revelation 7:12).

e. Black theology denies hell. With God dethroned, man can reconstruct a theology to the delight of the natural man who wants to have his cake and eat it too. He wants to live in rebellion against God with impunity. Biko said that pagan African religions have no hell and that Christianity must be seen in the light of that fact. He declares:

> There was no hell in our religion. We believed in the inherent goodness of man – hence we took it for granted that all people at death joined the community of saints and therefore merited our respect. It was the missionaries who confused the people with their new religion. They scared our people with stories of hell. They painted their God as a demanding God who wanted worship 'or else'.[27]

To reject the fact of hell is to reject clear New Testament teaching. Many passages deal with the subject (e.g. Matthew 5:30; 25:46; Luke 16:23; Revelation 1:18). The way to escape hell is through placing faith in Jesus Christ, and not by brushing aside biblical teaching on the subject.

f. Black theology is racialistic. Some advocates of black theology hold a view similar to that of the Black Muslims in the United States. Many American Black Muslims teach that black people are the only true human beings. Therefore, paradise is prepared only for the blacks, though a handful of 'human' whites might also be favoured. The thought of blackness and oppression so occupy the minds of black theologians that Jesus is limited to the black oppressed only. Moore writes along this line:

> Jesus as a Jew in first-century Israel was one of the poor, the colonised, the oppressed. Through the incarnation God identified himself in Christ with this group of people. Thus a meaningful symbol of God's identification with the oppressed is to say Christ is black.... Belonging to the oppressed, Christ is black.[28]

Black theology, along with other humanistic theological systems such as liberation theology, is anchored in the liberal understanding of the Incarnation, and in the liberal understanding of liberation. The Incarnation of our Lord is the assumption of humanity in general, and this includes both the rich and the poor, the oppressor and the oppressed, the black and the white. The classic passage on the Incarnation (Philippians 2:5–11) indicates that Jesus Christ became man in general. The form of a servant does not depict only a section of humanity; it indicates the vicarious suffering of the Servant of Yahweh (Isaiah 52:13–53:12) on behalf of *all* members of the human race, since 'all have sinned and fall short of the glory of God' (Romans 3:23). The Incarnation has made all men savable, but a person is saved only when he puts his trust in the incarnate Christ who died and rose again in order to reconcile men to God (1 Corinthians 15:3–4).

The concept of liberation is a confusing one today. Beginning with the promise that the oppressed are the object of Christ's mission, the liberal ecumenicals go on to limit the goal of Christ's mission to social, political, and economic liberation. If Christ came only for the downtrodden, in the narrow sense of the physically oppressed, why did He have any dealings at all with the religious leaders, the Pharisees; or the aristocrats, the Sadducees; or wealthy businesswomen, like Mary and Martha; or well-to-do fishermen, like the sons of Zebedee; or successful civil servants, like Matthew and Zacchaeus? Why did God allow His Son to be buried in the tomb of 'capitalistic' Joseph of Arimathea? If Christ's mission was for political liberation, why did He not organize a gang resistance to the Roman oppressors instead of urging His followers to go the extra mile (Matthew 5:41)?

While New Testament Christianity respects human dignity and calls for justice, liberation in terms of what Christ came to do must be understood as meaning liberation primarily from man's fundamental dilemma, which is sin. When Christ talked of freedom, the Jewish leaders thought of political freedom. But He made it plain that He meant freedom from sin (John 8:31–38). Both the oppressed and the oppressor need this message. The liberated person must, therefore, see his fellow men as equal before God. The heart of Paul's social ethics is summed up in Galatians 3:28: 'There is neither Jew nor Greek, there is neither bond nor free, there is neither male nor female; for you are all one in Christ Jesus'. The unity of believers will provide them a base from which they can launch out into a world which is full of problems and confusion.

Theology, which is the science of God and His creation, needs to be interpreted in such a way that it becomes meaningful to the listeners. The Bible addresses itself to the black man in his plight. It has done so in pointing out both the dignity and depravity of all men. It is the responsibility of Christian theologians to bring these facts to the knowledge of the public. If black theology is understood in that sense, then I am all for it. Unfortunately, black theology seeks to usurp the place of God's revelation. Its proponents have set up human experience as the basis for theologizing. Where biblical concepts are used at all, they are used only to support the preconceived notions of the theologian. I, therefore, see black theology as a worse danger than western liberalism. Rather than adhering to black theology, I appeal to my Christian brothers, Africans and non-Africans, to search the Scriptures, and stand by scriptural principles. According to the Bible, believers, under whatever human condition, are already liberated. 'For freedom Christ has set us free' (Galatians 5:1). But our freedom in Christ should challenge us to seek for justice through peaceful means. It is, therefore, not black theology we need, but the application of Christian theology to the black situation.

In the search of the African church for theological identity, evangelicals have a great potential for keeping the church biblical. Practically all the churches started out evangelical, and many of them are still evangelical. If adequate leadership is produced now within the evangelical sphere, the church in Africa will have a proper biblical perspective to hand on to forthcoming generations of African Christians. May the Lord help us all to experience the life of Christ, stand by His sure Word of truth, and proclaim it firmly and unmistakably throughout our continent, so that Africa may hear the voice of Him who is saying: 'Come to me, all who labour and are heavy laden, and I will give you rest' (Matthew 11:28).

NOTES

1 Bongeye Senza Masa, 'Reviving the Traditional Initiation School in Zaire' *AACC Bulletin* 8 (January–March 1975), 16.
2 For a more extended treatment of Christianity and African culture by Byang Kato, see his book *African Cultural Revolution and the Christian Faith* (Challenge Publications, PMB 2010, Jos, Nigeria, n.d.).
3 Bongeye Senza Masa, op cit.
4 J. K. Agbeti, 'African Theology: What It Is' *Presence* v (1972) 6.
5 Ibid.

6 John S. Mbiti, *New Testament Eschatology in an African Background* (London: Oxford University Press, 1971) 185.

7 Philip Turner, 'The Wisdom of the Fathers and the Gospel of Christ: Some Notes on Christian Adaptation in Africa' *Journal of Religion in Africa* iv (1971) 64–65.

8 Byang H. Kato, *Theological Pitfalls in Africa* (Nairobi: Evangel Publishing House, 1975).

9 'How Does Christ Set Free?' Paper No. 3, in *Structures of Injustice and Struggles for Liberation,* booklet 5 of *Notes for Sections,* Fifth Assembly of the World Council of Churches (Geneva: WCC, 1974) 31.

10 'Seeking Community: Where People of Different Faiths Live Together' paper No. 1, in *Seeking Community: The Common Search of People of Various Faiths, Cultures and Ideologies,* booklet 3 of *Notes for Sections,* Fifth Assembly of the World Council of Churches (Geneva: WCC, 1974) 14, 15, 17.

11 'Seeking Community: Where People Live in Cultural Crisis' Paper No. 5, in *Seeking Community,* booklet 3 of *Notes for Sections,* Fifth Assembly of the World Council of Churches (Geneva: WCC, 1974) 52.

12 Ibid.

13 'For the Liberation of the Indians,' *International Review of Missions* 60 (April 1971) 280.

14 Malcolm McVeigh, 'Sources for an African Christian Theology' *Presence* v (1972) 2.

15 Radio South Africa, June 17, 1975.

16 Steve Biko, 'Black Consciousness and the Quest for a True Humanity' *Black Theology: South African Voice,* ed. Basil Moore (London: C. Hurst, 1974) 39.

17 Ibid, 40.

18 Ibid, 47.

19 Basil Moore, 'What is Black Theology?' *Black Theology,* 5.

20 Steve Biko, 'Black Consciousness....', 43.

21 Basil Moore, 'What is Black Theology?', 6.

22 Ananias Mpunzi, 'Black Theology as Liberation Theology' *Black Theology* 137–38.

23 James H. Cone, 'Black Theology and Black Liberation' *Black Theology,* 48.

24 Ibid.

25 Moore, 'What is Black Theology?', 8–9.

26 Ibid, 9–10.

27 Biko, 'Black Consciousness....', 42.

28 Moore, 'What is Black Theology?', 8.

SUGGESTIONS FOR FURTHER READING

Byang Kato, *Theological Pitfalls in Africa* (Nairobi, Kenya: Evangel Publishing House, 1975).

Byang Kato, *The Spirits: What the Bible Teaches* (Achimota, Ghana: Africa Christian Press, 1975).

Byang Kato, *African Cultural Revolution and Christian Faith* (Jos, Nigeria: Challenge Publications, 1976).

Paul Bowers, '*Evangelical Theology in Africa: Byang Kato's Legacy*' *Evangelical Review of Theology 5:1* (April 1981) 35–39.

Other Books on the Bible published by ACP

God's message to the nation
Francis Foulkes

Amos – the book of Amos is brought alive for the modern reader. In this study of the book of Amos we can see the sins of various nations of the world today, sins of selfishness, godlessness, racism. We are made to realize how we need to look for ways in which the life of our nation may be made strong, pure and true.

Happy in trouble
Francis Foulkes

Philippians – this is a letter written when the apostle Paul was in prison, yet no letter of the apostle is more full of joy. It shows us the secret of true happiness and the secret of the apostle's joy and of his tremendous achievements as a missionary.

You could be rich!
Francis Foulkes

Ephesians – to many people this is the greatest and best-loved of all Paul's letters. It has much to say about the new life found in Jesus and how this new life has to be worked out in daily living.

Fight the good fight
Francis Foulkes

1 Timothy – the apostle Paul gives Timothy advice on church order, on qualifications for Christian leadership – and on the place of women in the church: matters of first-century importance with a twentieth-century relevance.

The three-fold secret of life
Francis Foulkes

1, 2, 3 John – Foulkes brings out clearly that John gives three tests for checking the reality of a person's Christianity. An Evangelical Literature Trust 'Pastors' Book Club' choice.

Revelation
Dr Harry Boer

The author is the former principal of the Theological College of Northern Nigeria and out of his wide teaching experience he leads the reader expertly through the intricacies of this book. It contains many fresh insights and shows how 'modern' the book of Revelation is for us today.

Watchman in Babylon
John Job

Ezekiel – the author is a former lecturer at Emmanual College, Ibadan, Nigeria. The main themes of the book are treated, and the overall pattern of this puzzling book is brought out clearly.

Also published by ACP

Survey of African Church History
Jonathan Hildebrandt

Provides a basic outline of the history of the Church in different parts of Africa, and demonstrates that Christianity is no recent arrival on the continent. Invaluable for all engaged in teaching church history in Africa.

Copiously illustrated with maps, diagrams and photographs.

The temptations of Jesus
Alastair Kennedy

Behind the scenes of our material universe, beyond the interplay of political forces, good and evil are locked in spiritual conflict. When Jesus met His enemy in the desert, this hidden warfare came into the open. The issue at stake was nothing less than the destiny of the universe, the ownership of each of our lives.

The Spirit's power
Stephen Smalley

The Bible's teaching about the Holy Spirit. A clear and balanced treatment of the subject, with a helpful section on the baptism and filling of the Spirit.

Elijah and Elisha
Dr Ronald S. Wallace

These two great Old Testament prophets are brought to life by the skilful pen of the author. The Old Testament is neglected by many preachers, but all will find helpful material here.